S0-ASJ-395

**PROPERTY OF
YARMOUTH TOWN LIBRARIES**

Sexual Abuse and Incest

Sexual Abuse and Incest

Dale Robert Reinert

Enslow Publishers, Inc.

44 Fadem Road   PO Box 38
Box 699   Aldershot
Springfield, NJ 07081 Hants GU12 6BP
USA   UK

SOUTH YARMOUTH LIBRARY
312 OLD MAIN STREET
S. YARMOUTH, MA 02664

Copyright © 1997 by Dale Robert Reinert

All rights reserved.

No part of this book may be reproduced by any means
without the written permission of the publisher.

Library of Congress Cataloging-in-Publication Data

Reinert, Dale Robert.
    Sexual abuse and incest / Dale Robert Reinert.
        p. cm. — (Teen issues)
    Includes bibliographical references and index.
    Summary: Explores the emotional, physical, and legal issues surrounding the crime
of sexual abuse, including possible reasons for committing abuse, how abuse affects
the lives of victims, and how society can combat sexual abuse.
    ISBN 0-89490-916-9
    1. Child sexual abuse—Juvenile literature. 2. Incest—Juvenile literature.
3. Sexually abused teenagers—Juvenile literature. [1. Child sexual abuse. 2. Incest.]
I. Title. II. Series.
HV6570.R45 1997
362.76—dc21   97-6704
                                                  CIP
                                                  AC

Printed in the United States of America

10 9 8 7 6 5 4 3 2

Cover Illustration: Enslow Publishers, Inc.

Contents

1

Learning About Abuse

The teenage years are a frustrating and confusing time. For some teenagers, including survivors of sexual abuse or incest, adolescence intensifies their feelings of confusion and frustration because their experience tells them to be wary, very wary.

In the last twenty years, the number of sexual abuse cases reported to police has skyrocketed, though most experts feel it remains a highly underreported crime. While more females than males are victimized, it is suspected that about 20 to 25 percent of all youth are sexually abused just before entering into or during the early part of adolescence.[1]

Sexual abuse occurs in Iowa and New York City, in Florida and Seattle, in Vermont and Los Angeles. It occurs among Caucasian Americans, and African Americans, and Hispanic Americans. It occurs everywhere and in all groups, and at about the same percentages. Sexual abuse has occurred over all time periods. Sexual abuse, illegal and inappropriate contact between non-family members—one of whom is usually a minor—and incest, sexual abuse between family members, can split families, create social and psychological problems, and affect society in many negative ways.

Candace's Story

Candace would take a shower every night before going to sleep. She would brush her hair two hundred times on each side. Each night, her bedtime ritual was a relaxing time. Whenever her mom had to work late or was out of town on business, her father would insist on brushing her hair. He would tell her how pretty she was, how "special" she was, how close they were. Her father would caress her shoulders and kiss her neck. After he would leave, Candace would take a very, very long second shower.

Who are the abusers and what are their motivations? Who are the survivors and how can they help themselves? How does society through the legal system, health care system, and schools prevent abuse from occurring and deal with it once it has been discovered? These questions are addressed in this book.

What Is Sexual Abuse?

Professor David Finkelhor in his book *Sexually Victimized Children* defines sexual abuse as the unwanted and/or uninvited sexual touching, patting, and talking that one person forces upon another.[2] *Boys and girls can be abused; men and women can cause abuse.* While this definition is broad, Finkelhor hopes that children and adolescents will learn that any unwanted contact is abuse. What follows are more specific examples and definitions.

The American Academy of Pediatrics released a pamphlet for parents in 1988 that summarized the definitions clearly:

> [Sexual abuse is] any sexual act with a child that is performed by an adult or an older child. Such acts include fondling the child's genitals, getting the child to fondle an adult's genitals, mouth to genital contact, rubbing an adult's genitals on the child, or actually penetrating the child's vagina or anus.[3]

Other, often overlooked forms of abuse occur. These include an adult showing his or her genitals to a child, showing the child obscene pictures or videotapes, or using the child to make obscene materials.[4]

When people confront sexual abuse and incest issues, the lack of a common definition often causes confusion, misunderstanding, and even more complexity.

In identifying abuse, Finkelhor, who has done a lot of research on the various kinds of abuse, describes three standards or ways to determine if a particular action a person chooses to take is abusive.[5]

First, he says, is the consent standard. A consent standard says that an act or a series of acts is abusive if a child or adolescent does not give his or her consent, a legal word for being able to give permission while understanding the potential consequences of making a choice. Sometimes a behavior will feel enjoyable while it is being experienced but then feels abusive only after it is over. Sometimes the feelings of abuse emerge years after the actual experience.

Finkelhor says that the age of the victim is the important second standard. The older the child, the greater the likelihood that he or she will have the ability to give permission to be touched. Wisconsin law, for example, says that someone over sixteen years old has the ability to give permission, while West Virginia law says that a fourteen-year-old adolescent is able to make the same decision. One other important consideration is a person's mental and emotional ability to make such a decision. After all, a fourteen-year-old who is pretty average has a higher ability to make a good, informed decision compared to a seventeen-year-old who is cognitively disabled.

The third and final standard, according Finkelhor, is called the community standard. The third standard answers the question, "What are the local and state laws in the area where the abuse occurred?" Investigators try to take into account the culture's values when performing an investigation. Police officers know that Hispanic and African cultures have different social rules about touch between adults and children, but they also know there are some forms of touch that are clearly not acceptable.

Community standards look at the age of the victim and the age of the perpetrator as well as the relationship between the two people. For example, some states have laws that say that if the age difference between the survivor and abuser is less than three years, then the abuse is classified as a lesser crime, while an age difference of more than three years causes the crime to be classified as more serious.

In every state, some acts between an adult and

a child are clearly seen as abusive. Sexual intercourse, for example, is always seen as inappropriate and deemed illegal, while other acts are unclear and questionable. For example, an adult who is purposely exposing his genitals to an eight-year-old in a park is clearly committing abuse, whereas an adult whose genitals are inadvertently seen by a child when the child and adult are changing clothes at the local pool is clearly not committing abuse.

Defining Sexually Abusive Acts

It is impossible to list every sexually abusive act. Remember, an abusive or incestuous act can be determined as such by answering three questions:

- ☐ Was the child/adolescent/teen able to make a good, informed decision?

- ☐ How does the age of the child/adolescent/teen affect the sexual experience?

- ☐ What are the laws of the city and state where the child/adolescent/teen lives?

It is less difficult to identify and confront abuse when the survivor does not know an abuser and when the abuse occurred randomly and only one time. When abuse continues over a prolonged period of time, it is called ritual abuse.

Legal Definitions

There are also legal definitions of sexual abuse. Most states have four or five different legal categories for sexual abuse. The types are usually called: child sexual offenses, incest, child protection statutes, sexual predator laws, and sexual assault laws.

Child sexual offense statutes include the criminalization of sex between children and adults, which is illegal in every state. The age of consent varies from state to state, with eleven being the youngest and seventeen being the oldest.[6] Most state laws say that sixteen or older is the age at which an individual has the capability to choose whether he or she wishes to share a sexual experience with someone or not. These laws were originally instituted to discourage sexual exploitation and promote "moral" attitudes among people. The longer laws are in effect, the more specific the wording and definitions

Sally's Story

Sally did not like her mother going to the store before supper because that was the time her stepfather would touch her breasts and tell her how "special" she was to him. He never seemed to do this thing at any other time.

become. That is because society gains in experience by which to govern itself.

Both sexual abuse and incest can include kissing; touching sexual parts like breasts, genitals, and buttocks; and sexual acts, including oral sex, anal sex, and vaginal sex.

So far, perpetrators have been talked about as being older persons, usually adults, but that does not have to be the case. Peers, or someone the same age as the abuse survivor, can also be a perpetrator, though this is rare. Usually, a five-year difference exists between peer perpetrators and their victims.

Why Do Abusers Do It?

Sexual abuse perpetrators have low self-esteem. Abusing children and young adolescents gives them a false feeling of being in control and having power. Very often sexual abusers feel they have no power and are not liked by anyone. To maintain the feeling of power and being in control, these abusers use threats, coercion, and lies to keep their victims silent. Strangers need to keep their victims silent only for a little while—a couple of hours or a day or two. Abusers who are well known to their victims, like parents or stepparents, use other tactics. For example, if a child or adolescent has been forced to have sexual intercourse with an adult, like his or her parent, the adult may threaten to tell the other parent that it was the child's fault. Other lies include threats of violence, such as "If you tell, I'll kill your mom," or "If you tell anybody, they're going to punish you," or "This happened because you made me do it—if anybody finds out, then you're really going to be in trouble."

Most men who abuse generally use their larger size and physical strength to get the child to do the sexual behavior and keep their secret. Men also use money, toys, and other powerful gifts to trick youngsters. When men abuse adolescents, they use many of these tricks, but they also use their ability to play on the victim's feelings for them.

Most women who abuse generally get their victims to feel sorry for them first. The abusive woman will talk about how lonely she is, how terrible her life is, and how she just needs to be close to someone. Some withhold their nurturance in order to get something sexual from the child. Boys are particularly susceptible to abuse by females during their adolescence because boys in many cultures are taught that it is a mark of their manhood to be sexually active.

Abusers use their knowledge of the laws to keep their victims quiet.

Telling the Secret

In the past, sexually abused children and adolescents never or very rarely told others about the abuse they experienced, and when they did tell, the "secret" was kept within the family. All too often these survivors received no help or emotional support.

Only in the past ten to fifteen years, as mental health and school counseling services have become more prevalent, the research clearer, public service announcements on television more common, and talk shows present on every channel, have children and young adolescents begun to reveal the "secrets" those who hurt them had made them keep.

Today when a child, adolescent, or teen tells of an abusive experience or series of experiences, the adults they tell are not only more likely to believe them, but those adults are more likely to do something to help bring the abuse to an end and to provide appropriate support.

Sexual abuse and incest have occurred throughout human history. Each culture has its own teaching about what kinds of touching are appropriate between adults and children. In most societies sexual contact between adults and children is taboo, or strongly against the rules, laws, and morals of society. In some cultures this inappropriate sexual behavior is never talked about. In most groups, people have only recently begun talking about sexual abuse as a problem that needs to be addressed with open communication and firm commitment.

How Many People Experience Abuse?

Ninety-five percent of sexual abuse and incest survivors know their abusers before the abuse begins.[7] According to the Federal Bureau of Investigation (FBI) only 5 percent of perpetrators, people who commit sexually abusive acts, are strangers to their victims. Fathers, stepfathers, brothers, uncles, grandfathers, male cousins, and other males commit abuse at higher rates than female relatives.

The FBI says one female in four and one male in five between the ages of eight and twelve experience some kind of sexual abuse or incest. Most sexual abuse occurs when the child or young adolescent is between the ages of eight and twelve. Generally, the abuse starts when the child is alone with either someone they know, like a parent or stepparent, or someone they don't know. Rarely do perpetrators attempt to harm a young person in front of others.

Frequency of Occurrence

Different research techniques used in studies of how much abuse occurs have gotten different results. One research technique has caused people to exaggerate their experiences. Another research technique has caused people to underreport sexually abusive experiences.

In research that involved face-to-face interviews, the percentage of individuals who claim to have survived sexually abusive experiences is very high. Researchers believe that face-to-face interviews give people the message that sexual abuse is very frequent, so people exaggerate their experiences.

On the other hand, written surveys tend to report very low rates of sexually abusive experiences, because people usually fear that others can read what they have written, so people underidentify their experiences with sexual abuse.

With differences in the studies' results, it is confusing for police, mental health counselors, and parents to fully understand how frequently childhood sexual abuse occurs. The most reasonable percentages seem to be between 28 and 38 percent of females and between 15 and 20 percent of males are sexually abused before the age of eighteen.[8]

There are three reasons for variances in these percentages. First, the researchers used different definitions of sexual abuse. Second, the researchers used different ways to gather information—either face-to-face interviews or written surveys. And third, the research populations varied by age.

How Is Sexual Abuse Different from Incest?

Incest is sexual abuse between two people who are related either through blood or marriage to one another. When incestuous abuse occurs, getting the abuse to stop becomes confusing and even more complicated.

There is a great deal of controversy and complexity about defining sexual abuse and incest. There are definitions that adults in schools and mental health agencies use and definitions that news media and television personalities and reporters use. This book will offer some clear definitions (see chapters 2 and 3) so the reader can better understand the issues involved when trying to understand sexual abuse.

When Victims Take Charge

Today's world is filled with negative role models, or examples, of how bullying someone results in the bully getting something he or she wants. Abusers take charge because they can use one of their strong abilities, like being big or being able to lie well or intuitively being able to trick trusting youngsters. Abusers believe they have the right to do what they do to their victims, and they convince their victims—at least for a period of time—that they deserve to be treated badly.

Victims do not deserve to be touched and threatened in the ways sexual abuse perpetrators hurt them. Sexual abuse victims who seek help and blame their abusers, not themselves, are called survivors, because they have recognized their pain and their innocence.

2

Abusers and How They Act

As mentioned in the previous chapter, sexual abusers tend to be men who know the child or adolescent with whom they are having inappropriate sexual contact. Although these men are usually heterosexual, or attracted to adults of the opposite sex, they frequently abuse children and adolescents of either gender.[1] Sexual abusers come from all races, socioeconomic classes, religions, and educational backgrounds. They are very skilled at getting the trust of both the children they intend to abuse and their victims' parents. While random abuse attacks happen, generally the abuser is someone well known to the child and his or her parents.

How Do Sexual Abusers Pick Their Victims?

Abusers spend a great deal of time grooming their victims, because this helps to reduce their risk of being caught. Neighbors and others who personally know the abusers often describe them as being well liked, and those same neighbors express disbelief when children make sexual abuse allegations. Often sexual abusers choose career fields that bring them into contact with a large number of children. Child sexual abusers often harm many children. Parents and children are encouraged to be suspicious of any adult who seeks to have an especially close relationship with a particular child or group of children.

The selection of the victim is no accident. Abusers seek someone who is vulnerable; gender is of little importance to many abusers, though sexual abusers who are homosexual do select their victims based on gender. Abusers try to spend a great deal of time with potential victims because they need to determine when and where they and the child are least likely to be interrupted.

Abusers tend to begin touching the potential victim in appropriate ways like horseplay, and then gradually begin to confuse and shift the boundaries of physical space until the child is unaware of what is really going on. Sexual abusers are planners and thinkers; they are constantly running the situation through their minds, increasing the chance that they can get away with the sexual abuse. The abuser also rationalizes that his or her deeds are acceptable because the victims need him or her or because they are in love.

However, it is truly impossible to describe sexual abusers in a manner that would allow us to know who is and who is not a sexual abuser. They can look clean or unkempt, wear nice clothes or ragged ones, talk violently or sweetly. The key characteristics can be confusing because they contradict one another. One key characteristic is the use of threats to maintain the secret of the sexual contact. The sexual abuser may also tell the child that what happened between them was the child's fault or that the child's parent will blame the child if he or she ever finds out what happened. Another characteristic is to keep what happened between them secret because their relationship is "special" and the feelings the abuser claims to have for the child are "special."

Sometimes the child finds the sexual activity to be pleasurable, which in turn causes a great deal of additional confusion. These children liked the contact but are confused because they have been told to keep the sexual contact a secret. The confusion is the result of being taught that there should be no keeping secrets from parents, especially in this case, where good feelings are associated with the experience.

Sexual abusers need to make sure their sexual contact with children remains a secret because that contact is illegal, immoral, and harmful to the child.

One clear way for children and adolescents to know whether to tell a secret or not is to check their feelings when told to keep a secret. Secrets accompanied by good feelings and the need to keep them for a limited time are, generally, good secrets to keep; for example, when a surprise birthday party is kept secret for a week. However, if a secret is accompanied by negative feelings, then the secret needs to be told. Tell an adult you

Ricky's Story

Ricky enjoyed sitting on the big hill in the park near his house. One day he saw a neighbor approaching him as he sat and enjoyed the warm summer weather. When the neighbor arrived at the top of the hill, he sat really close to Ricky and said things that made Ricky feel frightened. The man touched Ricky's private parts through his pants, and Ricky ran. The neighbor yelled a warning that Ricky had better not tell anyone or he would get in trouble, but Ricky knew this was something he had to tell about, even though he felt frightened about what his neighbor might do.

can trust about the secret. If that adult does not help, then the survivor of sexual abuse ought to keep telling adults until one of them is able to help.

What Motivates Sexual Abusers?

A number of things can motivate sexual abusers, including having been abused as children, low self-esteem, poor boundary development, extreme feelings of loneliness, and a need to feel in control of someone else.

Having been abused in childhood is one indicator that a person is at greater risk of abusing as an adult. Research shows that boys who have been abused between the ages of eight and twelve are three to four times more likely to sexually abuse a child as an adult than males who were never abused. Children who have grown up in a home or other environment where inappropriate touching and expressions of affection were permitted or encouraged may not as adults have an understanding of what is appropriate and inappropriate contact between adults and children. These sexual abusers believe their sexual contact with children or adolescents is an acceptable way of showing their feelings and building their relationships.

People who have been sexually abused, especially by a family member, learn that the abusive behavior is an acceptable way to be treated by those who supposedly care for them, like their parents. Often it is difficult for survivors to understand that they have been abused; they believe instead that such behavior is normal. When a sexually abused person gets older, he or she may actually look for dating and life partners who are sexually, physically, or mentally abusive.

Poor boundary development is often another characteristic of potential sexual abusers. Boundaries, like fences between neighbors' yards, are the limits of what is appropriate touching. For example, while it is appropriate for a three-year-old to sit on her father's lap while she repeatedly kisses her father, it is not appropriate in many cultures for a sixteen-year-old girl to do the same.

While every culture has its own rules for what is appropriate touching and what is not, every culture agrees that obvious sexual behaviors, like intercourse and oral sex, are not appropriate behaviors between family members. For example, Hispanic cultures are far more physically affectionate than Asian cultures, yet both find sexual acts between family members inappropriate and repulsive.

Many European-American cultures have embraced a strong male and weak female model as a way of teaching their children about boundaries. However, this model in many ways is no longer being taught by parents. Families now seem to be teaching their children that both males and females need to be strong and healthy, that effective communication and a sense of humor are more important in having a healthy relationship with someone than deciding who controls what part of the relationship. Individuals who sexually abuse are people who feel extremes. They feel weak, so they seek power and use coercion and threats to create a false sense of strength.

Young people should be familiar with their culture's rules about appropriate touching between parents and children, between brothers and sisters, between cousins, and between others. Knowing what their family believes is appropriate touching will help them determine if and when inappropriate touching occurs.

Persons with low self-esteem may also sexually abuse younger children or adolescents. When sexual abusers are in control of others a false sense of self-esteem gives them a temporary good feeling about themselves. This imagined sense of self-esteem disappears as soon as the sexual contact between them and the child ends.

In order to regain a sense of self-esteem they then use threats of violence to maintain some control over the sexual abuse survivor. For example, if an uncle forced his nephew to have oral sex with him, he may then threaten to tell the nephew's parents that it was the nephew's fault. Or the uncle may threaten to kill the nephew's parents if he tells anyone. Or the uncle may warn the nephew that his parents won't love him anymore if they find out. Very often the abuser has learned exactly what to say to create enough fear in the sexual abuse survivor to guarantee his or her silence—at least for a while.

Feeling extremely lonely is another risk factor for becoming a sexual abuser. When people feel disconnected from others, like having few, if any, friends; not having healthy relationships with family members; and not knowing how to initiate and develop close friendships; then the risk to them of becoming a sexual abuser increases. Such loneliness lends itself to being used to rationalize sexual contact as a deserving experience or as an experience that is appropriate because the adult and the adolescent are truly "in love." Sexual abusers who feel extremely lonely use childhood sexual abuse as a way to feel loved, desirable, and stable. Sexually abusing children becomes a powerful drive or obsession for the lonely sexual abuser, who mixes up being in love with being sexually inappropriate.

When a sexual abuser cannot continue his abusive experiences, he or she feels pain. To avoid the pain, he or she abuses again and again and again. Other emotions, like rage and anger, are also experienced by abusers when they are prevented from acting out their emotional illness.

While it is usually females who sexually abuse to meet emotional needs, this can also be one of the reasons behind sexual abuse perpetrated by males.

Feeling out of control can also motivate the sexual abuser. Sexually abusing a child or adolescent can be a power trip for the abuser. Forcing or making a person do something against his or her will may not only create a high for the abuser, but it may also create a situation where the child or adolescent is controlled in nonsexual ways in hopes of avoiding being sexually abused again.

Because abusers feel out of control much of the time, they find it easy to blame the victim. "If he would have just done what I told him to do, then I would not have had to have intercourse with him." "She wanted it. If she wouldn't have looked at me in that sexy way, I would have never been interested in her."

Cues and *triggers* are behaviors or signals that warn us that we may be entering into a troubled area. Like yellow lights at an intersection, cues and triggers help us to become alert and watchful of our situation.

Cues are hints that something is not right about the situation, and triggers are behaviors that either the child or adult does that forewarn of an abusive situation. An example of a cue might be a student going into the gym teacher's office and noticing that for the first time the teacher closes the door and draws the curtains. An example of a trigger might be being told how special you are as your teacher runs his fingers through your hair.

The Abuse Cycle

The abuse cycle can occur in what is referred to as ritual childhood sexual abuse. Ritual means that the abuse is not limited to a single isolated event, but that it happens at least several times over a longer time period, like a couple of weeks to a couple of years. About 30 percent of sexually abused children are ritually abused. The emotional impact of sexual abuse varies from person to person and is based on his or her understanding of the experience, the violent nature of the abuse, the duration and kind of activities the child was forced to perform, and at what age the abuse occurred.

For abuse that continues over a long period of time, there usually exists a cycle, or pattern. Initially, the abuser seems very kind and sweet to the child. The abuser gives him or her the attention the child may have been so desperately missing from his or her loved ones. The kindness progresses from gifts to hugs to inappropriate touches to fondling to removal of clothes to

Warning Signs

Here are some hints about determining whether you are or have been in a sexually abusive relationship as a child or young adolescent:

- ☐ Have you had a sexual experience with an adult or someone three or more years older than yourself?

- ☐ Has that sexual experience left you with awkward or negative feelings?

- ☐ Have you been in a sexual experience with a peer that left you with an awkward or negative feeling?

- ☐ Are the sexual experiences sealed with secrets or promises not to tell anyone about the experience?

- ☐ Does someone keep trying to get you alone?

- ☐ Are they telling you what you want when you really don't want it?

- ☐ Do they give you gifts for no apparent reason and then try to get affection in return for their generosity?

By asking these questions you will be able to become aware of an abusive relationship or experience. You will also be able to avoid getting yourself into difficult relationships or experiences by watching for cues and triggers. Being forced to keep experiences a secret is the biggest sign that something in the relationship is wrong.

performing oral sex and/or intercourse. The individual abusive acts end with the issuing of a demand for secrecy, whether it is issued through threat, guilt, blame, or kindness.

Through the use of threats sexual abusers get their victims to remain silent about the unwanted, illegal, though sometimes pleasurable acts they have performed with the survivor. The abuser may also offer bribes to the child or adolescent, particularly if he or she knows that the child does not receive very much attention and encouragement from his or her parents or other family members. The use of money or gifts serves to ensure that the illegal sexual acts will continue.

Very often the sexual abuse cycle is associated with a kind of sexual abuser called a pedophile. Pedophiles are sexual abusers whose main sexual expressions take place with children. They believe children are sexually mature and, therefore, can give consent. While this is not true, their perception, not reality, is guiding their behaviors.

3

Survivors and How Abuse Affects Their Lives

The main effect of long-term sexual abuse is low self-esteem, resulting from an inability to develop and feel secure in intimate relationships and express feelings appropriately or at all.

Survivors of Sexual Abuse

Very often, victims of long-term sexually abusive relationships in childhood feel completely worthless, while others feel that they do not deserve to be part of an intimate relationship. However, other survivors of sexually abusive childhood relationships enter into intimate relationships, including marriage, and allow themselves to reexperience more sexual abuse as well as other kinds of abuse.

Some children who have survived long-term sexually abusive relationships develop and mature into adults who have healthy relationships and who do not abuse others. Some children who have been victimized by long-term sexual abuse, however, are adversely affected for many years into adulthood. Their relationships, chosen professional fields, friendships, and outlook on the world are significantly changed by their experience.

The survivors who are emotionally secure know they are worthy of being loved and, therefore, do not enter into or remain in unhealthy relationships as adults. But many survivors of sexual abuse deal with the issue well into adulthood.

The Three Rules of Silence

Mental health professionals talk to their abuse-survivor clients about the three rules of silence because it helps those survivors understand why it has taken them so long to heal or why it has been so difficult to address the emotional and psychological issues surrounding their abusive experiences.

The rules are: You will not tell; You will not feel; You will not be aware.

You will not tell. Abusers use this rule to help guarantee that their victims will not tell anyone about the abuse. It is often phrased as instructions to keep their "special secret" because others would not understand their "special relationship." Abusers try to get their victims to believe that they must keep the abuse a secret, otherwise terrible things will happen to them and their loved ones. Abusers often tell their victims that they will be blamed for causing the abuser to abuse and that they will lose the love of their parents and relatives.

You will not feel. This rule subtly prevents the survivor from understanding how he or she really feels about the inappropriate contact between him- or herself and the abuser. This rule is often phrased by the abuser as "I can tell you really liked that," or "I know you like it." The abuser tricks the survivor into believing that he or she likes the physical contact, even though the survivor strongly doubts these false feelings. Many times the survivor's thought is "I must like it if it keeps happening."

The other issue that confuses feelings is the reality that some children and adolescents find the physical sensations of the abuse to be pleasurable even while the experience is emotionally and psychologically awkward. Sexual contact is pleasurable, but sexual contact can be inappropriate.

Signs of Sexual Abuse

Child sexual abuse may be defined as the misuse of children for the purpose of emotional and sexual gratification of an adult or older child who has power over the abused child. It can include physical as well as nonphysical contact. Below are the general physical and behavioral characteristics that are commonly demonstrated by sexually abused children.[1] Some of these signs may also be seen in nonsexually abused children.

Physical signs might include:

- irritation, pain, or injury to the genital areas
- fluid discharge from the vagina or penis
- stained or bloody underclothing
- frequent urination or pain when urinating
- unusual or offensive genital odor
- difficulty sitting or walking
- venereal disease

Behavioral signs might include:

- fearing a person or place once trusted
- regression to babyish habits, like thumb sucking
- clinging to trusted adults

- anxiousness or irritability that cannot be explained

- inappropriate knowledge of or attention paid to genitals

- acting out sexually or using sex talk

- fearful of having the mouth examined

- acting out sexually or abusively toward toys

- overcompliance

- nightmares and bed-wetting

- development of new fears

- development of eating disorders or unusual behaviors

- drawings that are scary

- acting overly mature, like an adult

- spending excessive time away from home and/or school

- refusal to participate in school and family activities

- significant changes in school performance

- hurting oneself verbally or physically, including suicide attempts

- running away

Expressing strong positive feelings for another person we feel affection for can be appropriate, but sexual contact between adults and children or adults and adolescents is never appropriate.

You will not be aware. This is the third rule of silence. Sexual abusers use threats and emotional games to trick sexual abuse survivors into not understanding what is happening to them. For example, many years after being sexually abused some children will tell stories of what happened to them and will clearly convey that they do not think of the sexual contact as abuse. This is particularly true of those who have been abused by women. Other adults will "remember" abusive relationships or events ten or more years after the abuse has ended. This forgotten abuse results from the adult teaching the child not to be aware of what has happened to him or her.

Damaged Self-esteem

Self-esteem is the way you feel about yourself. Do you feel that you are a person worthy of being loved and loving others? Do you feel that you are a good person who contributes in positive ways to the lives of friends and family members? Can you envision a future for yourself five, ten, and fifteen years from now? Do you smile more often than frown?

Lois's Story

Lois, fourteen, spent two weeks every summer at her uncle and aunt's farm in a nearby state. She enjoyed helping with the chores, watching the animals graze, helping pick mulberries, and walking in the fields. It was a nice break from the hustle and bustle of the city. This year, her uncle Colin seemed to be paying particularly close attention to her. One night, Uncle Colin invited Lois to take a walk through the woods. Lois agreed to a walk with Colin. During their walk, he talked a lot about what a beautiful girl Lois was becoming, which made Lois feel nice but also weird. The following summer, Uncle Colin touched Lois's breasts. And when she was sixteen, Uncle Colin made Lois take her blouse off as well as touch his genitals.

As a result of the three rules of silence, sexual abuse survivors experience damaged or broken self-esteem. Sexual abuse survivors are at greater risk for feeling inferior in their relationships and as such are more likely to put themselves down and enter into relationships that help these negative feelings to continue. The longer the sexual abuse continues, the more significant the sexual behaviors, and the more the three rules of silence are enforced, the more severe will be the negativity sexual abuse survivors will feel toward themselves.

Each person receives feedback from others about how his or her behavior is affecting others, but sexual abuse survivors have received the incorrect messages that they are the cause of the abuse, that they deserved to be hurt, and that their feelings are worthy only of being kept secret. If people get only negative messages from others, then they will give themselves only negative messages, and in turn, they will look to receive only negative messages from others. If they receive a positive comment, they will not know how to appropriately respond and may even disbelieve it.

One boy who was abused by his stepfather said:

> Before I was abused by my stepfather, I remember myself as being energetic and having lots of friends. But when my mom remarried and my stepfather starting making me have oral sex with him, I started to spend a lot of time alone. I avoided friends, didn't do homework, and suddenly felt like I couldn't succeed at doing anything difficult or challenging.

Another boy said, "I put up with the abuse because I wanted a dad like the other kids more than I wanted to feel safe and loved."

A young woman recollected the events leading up to her becoming a victim of sexual abuse:

> I remember my third grade teacher telling me how pretty I was, my fifth grade teacher complimented me on wearing a training bra, and my seventh grade teacher talked so nicely about my shape that when my gym teacher told me in eleventh grade that he had special feelings for me, it was easy to have sex with him when his wife was at work on Saturdays. It wasn't until college that I realized how sad my life was and how badly I felt about myself.

Although some adolescents do send sexualized messages to adults, these youths are not to blame. They have either learned to cope with the circumstances of their lives in such a manner or they have not been exposed to healthy role models. If a child or adolescent does send an overly flirtatious message or behave in a sexualized manner, and an adult responds to the message sexually by coming on to the child, then the youngster needs to ask him- or herself if this is the behavior he or she wanted from the adult. If not, then the child needs to clearly say so. Some children are simply having fun or are acting silly or are unaware of the potential danger of their actions, so it is important that they learn to act in a way to get what they really want from adults, which is usually affection, encouragement, and understanding, not sex.

Having healthy self-esteem is essential in today's complex and difficult world. A person with healthy self-esteem is not tricked by the three rules of silence or by the manipulations of abusers. Young people can recognize early on who is trying to damage their self-esteem.

Jennifer, a sixteen-year-old high school student who was sexually abused by her uncle during one of his visits, successfully survived the experience:

> Because my middle school counselor was a special lady, I was able to learn to like myself and to say nice things to myself when I reached little goals or accomplished something. Later on, in high school, I was able to tell which boys were nice and which weren't because the mean boys said some of the same negative things I used to say to myself.

Low Self-esteem Leads to Depression

The anger that results from inconsistent and confusing treatment by significant adults in a young person's life, like childhood sexual abuse, often manifests itself in adolescent or adult depression.

Mental health professionals talk to their clients about "stuffing" their anger down inside themselves. This anger, because it is not appropriately expressed and therefore released, builds up and causes other problems in life, like clinical depression and a tendency to form unhealthy relationships. In fact, anger turns into depression.

It is understandable how childhood sexual abuse survivors become depressed, since they have received threats and false messages, have been forced to keep powerful negative secrets, and have had personal boundaries violated by the very people they were taught to unquestioningly trust.

Depression can last a long time for some survivors of sexual abuse. When depression goes untreated for a long time, intense feelings of loneliness, hopelessness, and helplessness invade a person's life to the point of controlling his or her actions. The person is faced with a choice of either dealing with the depression through counseling, therapy, or the healthy support of others, or taking on new behaviors, called negative coping behaviors, like using drugs or alcohol to excess in an effort to dull the emotional pain.

When sexual abuse survivors effectively deal with understanding and accepting their experience, so moving on emotionally is possible, they are able to develop healthy self-esteem because they are able to experience their abilities and talents and feel pleased about their success. It is their healthy self-esteem that enables them to see false messages for what they are; to feel safe in the face of threats; to know which secrets are negative and which are positive, so they can keep the positive secrets and tell the negative secrets; and maintain their personal boundaries to preserve a sense of safety. Negative secrets are the kind that make us feel awkward and uncomfortable; positive secrets are the kind that make us feel happy.

Healing the Wounds of Sexual Abuse

While becoming emotionally healthy after being sexually abused begins with the survivor recognizing his or her pain, he or she cannot make the journey back to health on his or her own. Many sexual abuse survivors are helped by talking to mental health professionals like professional school counselors, certified professional counselors, psychiatrists, psychologists, and social workers.

Counseling is designed to help the sexual abuse survivor learn new and accurate information about being abused, while discovering things about his or her feelings and understandings. Many questions can be answered in counseling, for example: "How come I didn't say no?" "Why didn't my other parent protect me?" "Did I do anything to encourage the sexual abuse?" "How come I enjoyed some of the things we did?" "When will I get over this?"

Professional mental health counselors help childhood sexual abuse survivors understand their abuse experience, while teaching survivors new ways to protect themselves from future threats to their safety.

Professional help is not for the abused individual only. Very often, parents and other family members blame themselves for not picking up on the subtle cues that only hindsight reveals. In addition to seeking professional therapeutic help along with family members, teens and children may have the opportunity to participate in counseling groups where they can hear about and learn from the experiences of other sexual abuse survivors. Sometimes just knowing there are others who experience the same pain can be of great help.

What Is a Healthy Relationship?

In a healthy relationship, whether it is a friendship or a romantic relationship, each person wants the other to reach his or her full potential. Each person wants the other to find joy in other relationships, while not putting restrictions on who else each other can interact with. Both

Five Characteristics of a Healthy Relationship:

- ☐ Kindness
- ☐ Trust
- ☐ Expressing feelings
- ☐ Mutual support
- ☐ Ability to be oneself around the other person

Teen Survivors

Rochelle, a seventeen-year-old high school student, said, "Since my mom found out about my father making me have sex with him, she's been taking me to see a social worker. Before I started to see my social worker, I thought that everyone was moody and spent a lot of time alone in their rooms. Now I have learned new things about myself, which I guess I always thought were there but didn't know.

"I have doubted so much about myself. In counseling I have learned what is appropriate touching and what is not, and even though I don't see my father anymore I know what to look for in healthy relationships and what to avoid in unhealthy relationships."

★ ★ ★

Mikal, a fifteen-year-old athlete, said, "Before I started talking with my current counselor, I talked to my school counselor. He helped me figure out what was really going on with my soccer coach. Now if someone is saying or doing things to me I don't like, I can tell them to stop. My counselor says that's being assertive. I used to be either passive or aggressive and I'd always end up feeling hurt or getting in trouble. Being sexually abused made me moody, but now I know how to express my feelings, so I can stop someone from bothering me or encourage someone to be my friend."

★ ★ ★

Barry, nineteen, a junior-college student, said, "Before I went to group therapy, I didn't have anyone my own age to talk to about what had happened to me. Now some of the guys from the group and I are friends. We hang out and rely on each other. It's great to have someone to tell personal stuff to and have them say they understand exactly what I am saying."

★ ★ ★

Trisha, fourteen, a high school freshman, said, "The court ordered my parents to get me into therapy. At first, I didn't like it, but now I know my psychologist really does care how I am doing and whether I'm feeling sad or glad. She is working at helping me learn to make decisions for myself, and my parents have become supportive of me going to her."

persons celebrate each other's successes and try not to control each other's life choices, like where they go to college and who they build friendships with.

Healthy relationships do not require two persons to be together all the time. When they are together, it is because they want to be together, not because they need to be. Each person has healthy self-esteem and helps the other build more healthy self-esteem.

Kindness. Kindness means that the love people feel for each other is expressed through mutual respect for one another's feelings and through generous, unselfish behavior. Hurtful comments or suspicions or negative behavior indicate a lack of kindness.

Trust. Trust is a feeling most people develop very early in their life. Some researchers say it occurs as early as six months, others say before age five. Whichever it is, the fact is that most people develop good basic trust and then experience doubts about that trust when they are victimized by sexual abusers. Having such doubts is quite normal.

Trust in a relationship means that there is room for other friends and that those friendships do not take away from the relationship but rather add to it and strengthen it.

Being in a relationship with someone, whether

it is a friendship or a romantic relationship, means expecting to trust the other with one's feelings.

Expressing feelings. Learning to express one's feelings is important in our social world. Many mental health professionals teach their clients how to use "I statements." An "I statement" is a specific way to express how one feels, while avoiding making judgments about the other's motivations and behaviors. For example, instead of saying, "You always yell at me," an "I statement" would sound like this: "I feel hurt when I am yelled at. Please do not yell at me."

"I statements" conclude with a request for the other person to do something specific. While this method does not guarantee that the listener will do what is requested, it does allow a person to express a feeling. Using "I statements" can be helpful because people are sometimes unaware of how others feel.

The use of preset rules in communication helps

Expressing "I Statements"

I feel _____ when you _____.
In the future, I want you to _____.

to ensure that disagreements will not become fights. Setting clear rules about what is acceptable in disagreements, like no physical fighting, focusing communication on a current problem—not something that happened in the past—and no name-calling can help. Name-calling and physical fighting are ways to steer the disagreement off track. Staying focused on the topic of concern is important in bringing about a resolution.

Mutual Support. Mutual support in a healthy relationship means each person considers the other's interests as well as his or her own. Each recognizes that the other is going to have imperfections, but he or she can overlook them. Friends can count on each other, in good or bad times.

Able to Be Oneself. In a healthy relationship, both individuals are able to be themselves. They do not fear judgment or undue criticism from each other. They are not on the edge of their seats, waiting to be abused by their friend or partner.

4

Ending the Abuse

It is estimated that of the one child in four in the United States who is sexually abused, half of the survivors never tell, while many more tell but do not experience justice or healing. All too often families keep the abuse a secret, though it often does stop once it is discovered. Families often fail to deal with the trauma to the child in a healthy way.

Any sexual activity between a minor and an adult, from touching to intercourse, is illegal. Many people think that when a male adult sexually abuses a male minor, it is because the adult is homosexual and somehow either knows that the boy is going to grow up to be a homosexual or that the boy can be recruited to become a homosexual. Boys who have been sexually abused by adult males often fear they must be homosexual. While these feelings are real, sexual abuse survivors need to know that their abusive experience cannot make them either homosexual or heterosexual.[1] Homosexuality is determined by the presence of genetic markings that are present on specific genes.[2] Recent research indicates that homosexuality is not determined by someone's experiences, though boys who are molested are at risk for assuming they are homosexual regardless of their sexual orientation.[3]

Many sexual abuse survivors deny the painful experiences they have survived by telling themselves things such as, "This is no big deal." or "It's over and it's not going to happen again." or "It's best to forget it ever happened."

But sexual abuse survivors do not and cannot forget. They take memories and understandings with them into new relationships. Sexual abuse victims are affected by the abuse, whether they admit it or not.

Sexual abuse is never the fault of the victim. That is why most police and mental health professionals refer to victims as survivors. No one asks to be sexually abused, nor does one deserve to be sexually abused.

Ending an Abusive Relationship

The first thing a victim must do is tell a trustworthy adult. Professional school counselors, teachers, parents of friends, and adult relatives are good candidates. If the first person told cannot or will not help, which is rare, then the survivor should keep telling adults until he or she finds someone willing

Jileesa's Story

Jileesa was part of a new family; her mother remarried and now she had three brothers and sisters. It was quite an adjustment. Sometimes her mother would have to work late, especially around tax time and holidays. When her mom worked, she was watched by her new stepfather. He was nice enough, but he seemed to be more interested in his own children. One night, when her mom was working at the store, her stepfather came home. She could tell he'd had a few drinks. Jileesa went to her room because she didn't want to be around someone who was acting strangely. Her stepfather came into her room and sat next to her on the bed. He began touching her in inappropriate ways and saying strange things. Jileesa hated the touching and the smell on her stepfather's breath. Later Jileesa told her mother what had happened.

to help put a stop to the abuse and ensure that the problem is dealt with emotionally, at least, and hopefully, legally as well.

Dealing with the sexual abuse emotionally helps survivors relearn appropriate ideas of touch and healthy relationship rules, while also treating feelings of hurt, rage, and depression. Trained counselors can help with the emotional issues as well as explaining the survivors' legal options. Sometimes police can gather enough evidence to proceed without victim testimony, but it is generally best for the survivor to testify because it helps to bring some closure to the experience and strengthens the case against the alleged abuser.

Even if the sexual abuse is not reported to police, it is very important that mental health professionals become involved in healing the emotional injuries and in changing the behavioral coping strategies. Some families deal with the sexual abuse by, for example, having the parent who has perpetrated the abuse move out, obtain mental health counseling, and have only supervised contact with his or her victim.

Telling breaks the first rule of silence, and seeking mental health counseling helps to break the other two rules of silence. In order for the sexual abuse survivor to heal, the three rules of silence need to be broken.

Questions That Decide If Abuse Occurred

When you were a child or an adolescent were you ever . . . ?[4]

☐ touched in a sexual way

☐ shown or made to participate in sexual movies

☐ forced to listen to sexual talk

☐ made to pose for nude or sexually seductive photos

☐ forced to perform oral sex on another person

☐ anally or vaginally penetrated by someone

☐ touched, held, or talked to in a way that made you feel uncomfortable

☐ made to look at someone else's sexual organs

☐ told you were a good person only just before, during, or after having sex

Dealing with Emotional Issues

Professional counselors will explain the principle of confidentiality. All mental health counselors work under this principle, which prohibits them from telling others about what their clients tell them. While there are limitations to the principle of confidentiality, like having to tell when a client is going to hurt him- or herself or another, professional counselors discuss the limitations with a client during the first session. That way clients can decide what to tell and what not to. There are more limitations on freedoms and rights for minors than for adults.

Often parents have a greater right to know what has happened in counseling, but mental health professionals are skilled at informing parents about what was talked about while keeping the specifics about the sessions private. Sexual abuse survivors should ask their professional counselor about confidentiality during the first session.

Regaining a Sense of Happiness

Survivors of childhood sexual abuse experience powerful negative emotions, such as shame, embarrassment, fear, and self-doubt. Survivors feel shameful because there is an element of self-blame: How could I let someone hurt me in that kind of way? Survivors feel embarrassment: What will people think about me if they know what happened? Survivors feel fear: What if it happens again? How will I protect myself? Do I have to be around him again? Survivors feel self-doubt: Was it my fault? Can I say "no" and mean it? Did I mean it when I said it the first time?

Experiencing sexual abuse creates doubts for survivors in their safe and healthy relationships as well as in their other relationships. Survivors fear telling their story because they might be blamed or because their friends might stop being their friends. They worry about their ability to protect themselves, their parents' ability to protect them, and that they may never trust as freely again.

Childhood sexual abuse leaves the survivor feeling powerless. Feeling powerless creates conflicting and out-of-control emotions. When a person's most personal and intimate boundaries have been violated, it is natural for him or her to feel he or she has lost control over his or her life.

Years after the abuse, it is possible to have vivid memories of the experiences or general anxiety and depression.

How to Become Self-Aware and Avoid Self-Blaming

Given that survivors experience strong negative emotions as aftereffects, it is important for survivors to remember that they have survived and that regaining a sense of self-protection, though difficult, is possible. The key to developing a sense of self-protection is strengthening the sense of self-awareness.

Being self-aware means understanding one's body and one's emotional needs. When someone is getting too close or invading a person's psychological safety zone, which varies for each person and by culture, the body will automatically react by trying to create greater distance between the two persons. If moving away is not successful at increasing the space, then the body will respond with an increased heart rate and sweaty palms and forehead. At this point it is necessary to speak up.

Using "I statements" can be helpful in restoring your personal space. Simply say, "I feel crowded when you stand that close, please back away." Jon, a fourteen-year-old survivor, said, "I tell people right away if they are standing too close to me. At first, I would get excited and say it too loudly or out of the blue, but since I have been saying it for almost two years, I've become comfortable asking people to respect my space."

Saying no is also important. If a minor is approached by an adult for sex, the minor should say no and immediately start screaming. Throwing such a tantrum is often enough to dissuade the abuser. If a stranger asks a young person to get into his or her car or to let him or her into the house, there are two things to do. First, the young person should say no. Second, the young person should tell a nearby adult. For example, Kelly was able to stop a stranger from sexually abusing her. When she was approached in the park by her house, she immediately began screaming and ran to the edge of the park. A store owner heard her screams and called the police. The stranger was arrested just a few miles away. The police, the store owner, and her parents praised Kelly for her quick reaction.

Anyone who feels uncomfortable around any adult for any reason ought to do whatever is needed to get out of the situation safely or to bring others into the situation. He or she should speak up. Safety is much more important than trying to save an adult's feelings. It is better to be clear and remain safe than to risk being hurt.

A sexual abuse victim has the right to become a sexual abuse survivor; talking about the experience and learning new skills and strategies will make such a transition successful.

5

Legal Issues

$\mathcal{A}$lthough more childhood sexual abuse is not reported than is reported, families often choose to attempt to address the problems and issues surrounding the sexual abuse privately. In addressing the issues privately, families risk not dealing with the effect the abuse has on the family, particularly if the abuser is one of the parents or if the abuse has been going on over a long period of time.

Pitfalls of Resolving Sexual Abuse Privately

Oftentimes, the parents' need to deny their failure to always protect their child leads to an end of the abuse but not to a beginning of the healing and recovery process.

Recovering from sexual abuse is a long and difficult process. If competent professionals specially trained in dealing with sexual abuse are not part of the family's dealing with the abuse, then the recovery cannot be complete. Simply put, parents and children do not know enough about the effects of sexual abuse to help themselves recover in a healthy manner, and while involving priests or ministers is helpful, unless they have specialized training in childhood sexual abuse issues, the recovery will not be complete.

Resolving Sexual Abuse Through the Legal System

While it is up to sexual abuse survivors to decide to cooperate with the police once allegations are made, the more sexually abused children and adolescents cooperate with the police, the more sexual abusers will be caught, convicted, and serve time in prison. Survivors also need to remember that their silence may encourage abusers to inflict the same painful experiences on others. But what may be the most helpful part of seeking legal justice for the painful sexual contact is the psychological closure. This kind of closure may help the survivor fully recover.

Chung's Story

Chung, a new kid in the neighborhood, was playing catch with some friends in the park. After tossing the ball around for a while, he and the other boys went to the refreshment stand, where they all bought shakes. A man, who the other boys knew as Mr. Ryan, approached. They all said hello and Mr. Ryan sat down next to Chung. Mr. Ryan told stories and made the boys laugh, especially when he put his glasses on upside down and stuck french fries in his nose. A few minutes later he invited the boys over to his house to go for a swim in his new pool. He didn't live very far, and he had plenty of swimsuits. The boys went swimming and had a great time, except Chung who wondered why Mr. Ryan had to watch the boys change from their clothes into the swimsuits and then again later when they needed to dry off. The other boys thought it was no big deal, but Chung was concerned, so he talked to his dad about it.

Although dealing with sexual abuse through America's legal system may be helpful in bringing final closure to the experience, it will not be an easy endeavor. For example, while it is helpful to talk about the abuse, reporting it to the police could result in having to tell and retell what happened, when it happened, how it happened. It means being challenged by an attorney who will try to prove the accuser wrong. It means having to tell strangers, either a judge or a jury, what happened, and telling strangers about painful experiences is always more difficult than telling adults one knows and trusts, which is difficult enough.

In filing a report, police officers will interview the victim and the others concerned. If the person is a minor and lives in the same house as the alleged perpetrator, the police may ask the perpetrator to leave the home until they can get to the bottom of what happened. In some cases, the police will call Child Protective Services to place the minor in the care of safe adults, but, generally, Protective Services and the police try to keep immediate family members together.

Honesty is most important for a successful investigation. Children who have been sexually abused will need to tell police the exact sexual acts that were forced upon them. Naturally, telling strangers such things can make a person feel embarrassed and awkward. Remember, however, the adults involved in the investigation and court case are there to judge the alleged perpetrator, not the victim.

A minor has the right to testify in the judge's chambers instead of the courtroom, and the right to determine if his or her parents should be present during his or her testimony. In some states, like New Jersey, new laws are being introduced that require the police authorities to tell the survivor when the sexual abuse perpetrator is being released from prison. Police authorities are also required to tell the residents of the neighborhood where the molester is going to live. This law, sometimes called Megan's law, will be discussed later in this chapter.

Understanding the Court Proceedings

Based upon the victim's police report, the police talk to the alleged molester—if he or she is a stranger, which is rarely the case, then the report is kept on file as the police investigate similar reports. For example, in one highly publicized case in Chicago, Illinois, a suspect was arrested by police during a routine traffic check because his van, which had a large crack in the windshield, matched the description of the vehicle driven by a man who had molested three girls, ages eleven, twelve, and fourteen. The three survivors were able to pick him out of a lineup and a search warrant garnered three personal objects taken by the alleged molester.

The allegations the victim makes will be checked for accuracy; for example, for location and time. Once police officers are finished with their investigation, they share the results with the district attorney's office, where prosecutors will determine if there is enough evidence to proceed to court or if other evidence will need to be collected. If lawyers for the government decide to move forward with the case, then the first step is to make an arrest, file charges, and hold an arraignment, a legal proceeding where the charges are publicly made against the perpetrator.

After an arraignment, a hearing is scheduled in which the essential details of the case are presented and a judge determines if there is enough evidence to proceed to trial. Rarely are cases dismissed in the hearing stage, because prosecutors will not proceed with charges if there is not enough evidence to insure a trial. However, even if there is enough evidence to proceed to trial, there is no guarantee that there is enough evidence to get a conviction. Winning a conviction requires a higher standard of evidence than a hearing. The victim may be asked to testify at an arraignment and will testify during the trial.

Many times, between the arraignment and the start of the trial, many alleged molesters, based on the advice of their attorney, will agree to a plea bargain, or agreeing to plead guilty to lesser charges. While this saves the victim from having to testify and saves the government money and the molester public embarrassment, it also means that he or she will spend less time in jail, perhaps six months in prison instead of ten years.

If the case proceeds to trial and the suspect is convicted, then a sentencing hearing is scheduled. While juries may determine if a suspect is guilty or innocent, a judge determines the length of time the molester will spend in prison.

New Laws Try to Solve the Problem

Megan's Law. This law is named for a young New Jersey girl who was raped and murdered by a pedophile who was living in her neighborhood after being released from prison. The law, which was originally passed in New Jersey and has been passed by numerous other states, requires that police authorities inform residents of a neighborhood where a child sexual abuser will live upon leaving prison. The idea behind the law is to protect the neighborhood children by warning parents and other community members prior to a child molester's release, thereby allowing them to prepare children with good protective skills. However, critics of the law charge that, having paid his or her dues to society by serving a prison sentence, the ex-convict deserves to be given the benefit of the doubt. After all, how will the newly released pedophile be able to move on psychologically if his or her

The Legal Degrees of Sexual Assault

☐ *First Degree Sexual Assault.* Anyone who has sexual contact or sexual intercourse with someone younger than thirteen can be found guilty of first degree sexual assault, a class B felony.

☐ *Second Degree Sexual Assault.* Anyone who has sexual contact or intercourse with someone younger than sixteen but at least thirteen can be found guilty of second degree sexual assault, a class C felony.

☐ *Failure to Act.* Anyone who has knowledge of illegal sexual activities involving children and fails to act can be found guilty of a class C felony.

☐ *Incest with a Child.* Anyone who either marries or has sexual contact or sexual intercourse with a child who is related to him or her as close as a second cousin or closer, including being related through adoption, can be found guilty of a felony appropriate for his or her abuse. Most states use the child sexual assault laws when prosecuting alleged incestuous molesters, because there is usually no extra penalty for incest.

☐ *Sexual Exploitation of a Child.* Anyone exploiting a child by forcing him or her to watch or participate in sexually explicit conduct can be found guilty of a class C felony.

The *statute of limitations* is the legal amount of time in which a survivor of a crime has the right to bring criminal charges or file a civil suit against a perpetrator. When a crime is reported to police, the case is forwarded to the district attorney after the investigation. The district attorney determines whether to file charges. If the statute of limitations expires before charges are filed, then the survivor cannot use the legal system as a way of seeking recourse. Civil cases have shorter time limitations than criminal. Criminal cases require more evidence and a unanimous jury decision, whereas civil cases have a lighter burden of proof.

In criminal cases, the statute of limitation is generally six years for felony cases and three years for misdemeanor cases. First, second, and third degree sexual assault are usually considered felonies, and fourth degree sexual assault is considered a misdemeanor.

Some states have extended the time frame of the statute of limitations in order to facilitate prosecutions. If a child is abused before the age of sixteen, some state laws allow the person to file charges until his or her twenty-sixth birthday; that is, more than ten years after the abuse has occurred.

The statute of limitations can last as long as fifteen years if a therapist or doctor abuses a child in his or her care. While these increasingly longer periods of time seem to be encouraging, it is particularly distressing to learn that the shortest statute of limitations applies to those who are the most frequent abusers. Family members who sexually abuse children must have charges filed against them within two years after the end of the abusive acts.

Laws vary from state to state. Your local library should have reference material covering the laws of your state.

neighbors condemn, harass, and prejudge him or her? Several halfway houses have been burned down by neighbors who do not want child sexual molesters living in their community. These citizens fail to understand that such molesters are already living, undetected, within their community.

The Three-Strikes Law. This attempt at becoming tough on criminals requires that some criminals serve life in prison without parole if they are convicted of three felonies in three separate crimes. While most of the felonies qualifying for this new law are drug related, some are sex crime laws.

Sexual Predator Laws. This attempt to prolong the time that convicted child molesters serve currently exists in only a few states. Based on an examination of the molester, a state-qualified psychologist determines if the molester has undergone significant rehabilitation. If the report indicates that attempts at rehabilitation have failed, then a judge can order the molester to enter a mental facility for the purpose of undergoing psychological treatment in an attempt to rehabilitate the molester prior to release back into the community. Six states currently have sexual predator laws: Arizona, California, Minnesota, New Jersey, Washington, and Wisconsin.[1]

Sexually Abused Children's Bill of Rights

The Children's Forensics Institute urges the adoption of the "Sexually Abused Children's Bill of Rights" by every state to help ensure that child victims are not further harmed by the American legal system.[2] This Bill of Rights has been adapted by the author as follows:

- The sexually abused child will not experience any forced contact with his or her abuser.

- Custody of sexually abused children shall always be determined by what is best for the child, not by what is best for the parent.

- Every judge shall complete a training program on the diagnosis and treatment of child sexual abuse.

- In all proceedings addressing the alleged sexual abuse of children, evidence that the abuser has abused another child shall be admitted.

- Courts shall keep an open mind in determining the value of new evidence.

- Competent expert testimony that the child is a survivor of childhood sexual abuse trauma shall be admitted in every court proceeding involving the welfare of the child.

- The testifying trauma shall be minimized through the use of closed circuit television testimony and admissibility of the child's other statements given to police investigators and mental health counselors.

- The abusive parent shall pay all court costs and costs of therapy incurred by the innocent parent.

- No innocent parent shall be charged with contempt if that parent prohibits the abusive parent from seeing the child if he or she has reasonable grounds based on competent testimony.

- Any innocent parent charged with contempt shall have a full public hearing.

How Does Parole Work?

Parole is the process developed in many states to release convicted criminals from prison before they have served their entire sentence. The average jail time served is two thirds of the sentence, which means that if a sentence is ten years, then about six or seven years will be spent in prison. Paroling inmates originally was intended to reward good behavior in prison and motivate convicts to become rehabilitated. Today, many states use parole to relieve prison overcrowding.

However, many studies have shown that nearly 80 percent of those prisoners released early are rearrested within two years of their release. Several states have begun to limit the kinds of crime that have parole options; usually, violent crimes are excluded while crimes called "white collar" are included.

If someone qualifies for parole, it is because a board appointed by the state's governor reviews a prisoner's file, listens to prison-employee testimony about the conduct of the prisoner, looks at the severity of the prisoner's crimes and the remorse expressed by him or her, and listens to the pleas of the victims' families. After taking into account all the information, the parole board makes a decision about a prisoner's release.

Because the last thirty years have seen huge increases in violent and sex crimes, and because of the high rates of child molesters repeating their crimes on new victims, a movement has emerged whose purpose is to change the way courts deal with childhood sexual abuse, the children involved, and the families affected by the trauma that accompanies the sexual abuse.

6

Moving on Emotionally

A survivor selecting a professional counselor should ask the person some questions. Here are some examples: What training in sexual abuse counseling has he or she received? Has he or she ever been abused? How has the counselor addressed his or her own feelings about childhood sexual abuse? If a child is seeking the assistance of a professional counselor, then a parent will usually ask these questions, but if an adolescent is seeking therapy, then wisdom dictates that the adolescent should at least be present when the parent asks the questions and maybe even ask some of the questions him- or herself.

What to Expect from a Mental Health Counselor

Therapists who have worked with sexually abused children and adolescents and their families will share much or all of the above information with their clients during the first session, so the survivors and their families begin to become familiar with and trustful of the therapist.

During the first session, clients are asked a series of questions—many of which are standard for every person seeking professional counseling, but some of which are specific to sexual abuse survivors. They include whether anyone has touched the client in an inappropriate way, and whether the survivor has begun dealing with any of the memories or experiences or feelings about the abuse.

For adolescents much of the first counseling session may be spent having the counselor talk, while children may interact with the counselor by completing various tasks like playing house or games, drawing or painting, and building things.

While much of the talking is probably going to be done by the counselor during the first session, the client should not be afraid to ask questions and share thoughts. Asking a question helps one to get to know and understand the therapist, and getting to know him or her will help one begin the process of healing emotionally. Therapists are willing, safe professionals to be trusted; trusting a therapist will help to reinitiate the process of trusting others, as well as trusting oneself.

Being sexually abused often leaves a young person feeling vulnerable, and mental health counselors offer survivors a chance not only to trust again but also to feel emotionally stronger.

Why It Is Important to Talk to a Counselor

Children and adolescents who enter therapy will learn how to protect themselves in the present and future. They learn to seek the company of others when they are alone with someone who is making them feel uncomfortable with his or her words or actions. While a survivor acknowledges that he or she cannot control everything in his or her environment, survivors learn to be aware of and alert to any dangerous situations and the cues that indicate the approach of those situations.

Survivors learn to communicate to their parents where they are going to be spending their time and with whom their time will be spent. Survivor children learn to play in groups, and adolescents learn to socialize in groups of friends their parents know. Parents learn to get to know their child's friends and the parents of their child's friends. They learn not only their names, where they live, and the work they do, but also the

Jean's Story

Jean hardly ever thought about the terrible things her father did to her at the cabin. She had known from the beginning that she was not to blame and that she would be fine. She didn't know why she had such confidence in herself but she did. Today, finally, she was going back to the cabin alone. It was the first time since the abuse ended, since her father moved out, since her mother sued for divorce, and since she finished talking with a counselor that she had been to the cabin. She decided she wanted to go back and spend some time alone there, so she would know that she could be safe in even the places where she was hurt.

values taught in the family, the behaviors expected from both adults and children, and the rules about secrets within the family.

Adolescents who have survived sexual abuse allow their parents to check up on the adults in their lives; for example, coaches, teachers, scout leaders, church volunteers, bosses, and others will be met by parents.

In therapy, survivors learn to identify who they can and cannot trust. Survivors also learn to protect their own safety.

Learning about safety is a lifelong process in

which everyone participates. Rules about how to ride school buses, cross streets, use knives, and even tie shoes deal directly with safety. After surviving a sexually abusive relationship or experience, children and adolescents need to learn or relearn appropriate touch boundaries; for example, young survivors may be taught not to let an older child or an adult take off their clothes, while adolescents may be taught how to communicate with boyfriends or girlfriends about what they are comfortable with regarding touch.

Therapists are easy to talk to because they are trained to help others talk about difficult subjects. They use language appropriate for the age of their client. Professional mental health counselors create a safe, calm environment where survivors relearn to trust adults.

Children learn to understand that there are some adults who cannot control themselves; for example, alcoholics cannot control their drinking without learning new behaviors, and some adults lose control over their tempers, so they, too, need to learn new, appropriate behaviors.

Survivors learn that molesters are the exception rather than the rule among adults. Therapists help reacquaint survivors with adults who are kind and warm and understanding without looking for something in return.

Possible Issues to Deal with in Counseling

There is no specific set of psychological issues that every childhood sexual abuse survivor needs to address. Every individual will experience a different understanding of the abusive experience and will therefore have to deal with his or her own issues; however, some common elements can be summarized in the following eight topics:

☐ Learning how to set, and demonstrating achievement of, large and small goals

☐ Learning to redirect the negative coping behaviors into positive coping behaviors

☐ Learning how to establish and reinforce social connections

☐ Developing ways to talk about and break down the harmful secrecy that can exist in families

☐ Symbolically or actually confronting the sexual abuser

☐ Understanding and expressing that recovery is an ongoing process

☐ Creating a new understanding of the abuse to help others

☐ Breaking the three rules of silence

Breaking the three rules of silence and undoing the isolation suffered as a result of sexual abuse can be achieved through at least six different ways, including telling one's story, forming an appropriate therapeutic relationship, entering into a support group with other sexual abuse survivors, identifying and sharing feelings, talking about and learning how to reduce shame and guilt, and accepting that one is not alone in one's experiences.

Grieving

A child's understanding of his or her abusive experience is related to how his or her parents react. The period of time after the abuse ends is difficult for both parents and children. Parents grieve over the loss of their success at protecting their children; children grieve over the loss of their innocence, their boundaries, and their capacity to trust others. While parents grieve each and every day, healing bit by bit over time, children grieve for a moment here and a day there. It may take the child much longer to resolve his or her feelings. For example, children will need to talk about the abuse over and over, but adults will feel that they have dealt with their feelings and put it behind them.

Moreover, adults become confused by a child's unwillingness to talk about his or her experience when the adult wants him or her to talk, but the child will likely bring it up without warning and out of context. It is on these surprise occasions that adults become frustrated by the child's age-appropriate process of grieving and healing, especially if the adult has already dealt with his or her own grief.

Common Problems Experienced by the Survivor

The most common problems of survivors include anxiety, confusion, depression, and low self-esteem. However, individuals who exhibit these symptoms ought not to automatically conclude that they have experienced sexual abuse. These symptoms can be attributed to a wide variety of stressors, some of which are characteristic of sexual abuse.[1] Other frequent problems include the following:

- having a poor or negative body image
- feeling childish without reason
- demonstrating addictive behaviors, like alcoholism and drug abuse
- becoming a victim of other abusers
- feeling like two or more different people
- becoming either an abuser or a person who tries to protect children
- overachieving or underachieving
- failing to maintain intimate and/or romantic relationships
- feeling isolated and alone
- startling easily
- feeling uncomfortable with being touched or demonstrating obsessive-compulsive sexual activity or impotence
- showing violent behavior or an irrational fear of violence
- having memory flashbacks
- suffering from insomnia
- having nightmares
- feeling excessive guilt and/or shame

Ten Things That Will Help a Survivor

Here are ten things sexual abuse survivors can do to help themselves during their recovery process:[2]

1. Accept that the abuse was not their fault and recognize that they are responsible for helping themselves heal.

2. Read books and pamphlets about childhood sexual abuse, but not just at one time. It is important to read about the subject in childhood, in adolescence, and throughout adulthood, because the issues of sexual abuse affect survivors differently throughout the stages of their lives.

3. Go to therapy with a professional counselor who has specific training in childhood sexual abuse issues and attend a survivors' support group.

4. Learn to talk about sexual abuse with close friends and family. Telling needs to be done in an appropriate time and place.

5. Acknowledge that healing is a long process, survivors will experience strong negative emotions, and that those emotions may resurface periodically throughout their lives.

6. Suicidal thoughts are common among sexual abuse survivors, and such thoughts require mental health attention. Thoughts about hurting oneself generally dissipate as one deals with emotional issues surrounding sexual abuse.

7. Listen carefully to what an adult who knows a lot about abuse says. He or she has knowledge

and can give survivors information that leads to understanding the abusive experiences.

8. Affirm and show love. Take one day at a time, demonstrating patience with themselves. Continue relationships with people who are kind and positive.

9. Become involved with a volunteer group that works with survivors. Seeing other survivors in different stages of recovery can be very helpful.

10. Think very carefully about their sexuality. Learn what warm, kind touch is; learn what healthy sexual expression looks and sounds like; examine how the abuse has affected their sexuality; and establish guidelines to follow involving sex.

Survivors Talk About Healing and Moving On

Despite a long process of recovery, most sexual abuse victims do recover. While the process of recovery differs for everyone, many of the same issues are dealt with, though in a different order or in a different way. The following tasks are addressed by most survivors during their recovery, though every survivor may not need to deal with every one of these tasks.

First, sexual abuse survivors need to make a decision to get better, or heal. They have recognized that their coping mechanisms are no longer getting their needs met, so they seek help in dealing with their abuse in order to learn new and more effective behaviors, feelings, and understandings. Significant healing occurs only when a survivor chooses it and works hard to change his or her way of coping.

Sometimes healing begins with an intensifying of negative feelings and memories. Things seem to get worse instead of getting better, because many, if not all, of the feelings the survivor has been stuffing down inside him- or herself are beginning to surface. It is these negative feelings that make the beginning of the healing process difficult. The key to getting through this part of healing is to remember that the intense negative feelings are only temporary and will pass in a few weeks.

Survivors then begin to remember either the actual experiences, if they have blocked or purposely forgotten the experiences, or the feelings brought about by the abuse. Remembering is important because it helps the survivor learn how to experience feelings again, including real, positive emotions.

Usually at this point of the recovery process, especially for adults finally dealing with their issues, survivors doubt that their memories and feelings are accurate. But in coming to believe their experiences and their perceptions, recovering adults begin embracing themselves because they acknowledge that they were really, truly hurt by the abuse.

Only about half of abused children tell someone about it within a week of it happening. If the abuse is not reported then, it is usually kept a secret until adulthood. Telling someone about the abuse can be a powerful healing force in a person's life. It also helps to dispel the idea that the child needs to be ashamed because somehow he or she wanted the sexual activity to happen.

While children usually believe the sexual abuse was their fault, adult survivors are able to appropriately place the blame on the adult abusers because they more fully understand the amount of trust and reliance children need and seek from adults.

One coping mechanism or skill for sexual abuse survivors is losing their sense of vulnerability, which means that they are forced to grow up too quickly. Part of recovery helps survivors reconnect with their lost child because such a connection helps them feel anger at the abuser and compassion for themselves.

It is only after regaining a connection to their inner child that survivors can begin to trust themselves again. In learning to listen to their own inner voice, they find a friend and a guide who can help them continue to heal. If a child has been sexually abused and no adult believes his or her story, then the child will come to doubt his or her own feelings, perceptions, and intuition. For adult survivors, reconnecting to their inner child helps them learn how to trust themselves again.

Grieving is the next part of recovery. It allows survivors to honor their pain, let their pain go, and finally move into the present.

Anger, often a negative force in survivors' lives, is changed into a power that focuses and motivates. Therapy helps survivors learn how to direct their anger both at the appropriate person and in appropriate ways.

Confronting the abuser, whether directly or through therapeutic techniques, is helpful during the recovery process. Confrontation can be a phase of healing that results in leaps of growth. In therapy two ways survivors can confront their abusers are: to pretend the abuser is sitting on a chair opposite them, and to write letters to the abuser.

Following confrontation is forgiveness. These two parts of the healing process are often closely connected. The important part of the forgiveness process is not forgiving the abuser but forgiving oneself. Sexual abuse teaches the abused to treat themselves badly, and to doubt and harm and insult themselves. Healing requires that survivors forgive themselves for the harm they unknowingly inflicted upon themselves.

Moving through these parts of the process repeatedly, the survivor will at some point discover that his or her feelings and attitudes have stabilized. He or she will have resolved what the abuser did and what part family members may have played. Survivors do not forget their experiences, but they do move on from the abuse and allow positive experiences to direct and influence their lives.

Where to Find Help

National Youth Crisis Hotline
1-800-448-4663

National Domestic Violence/Abuse Hotline
1-800-799-SAFE
1-800-799-7233
1-800-787-3224 TDD

Alabama

National Resource Center on Child Sexual Abuse
107 Lincoln St.
Huntsville, AL 35801
800-543-7006

Arizona

Sexual Assault Recovery Institute
3625 N. 16th St.
Phoenix, AZ 85016-6443
602-235-9345

Arkansas

Abused Women and Children's Shelter
1419 Hunter St.
Arkadelphia, AR 71923-4736
501-246-2587

California

Abuse Services Center
1589 W. 9th St.
Upland, CA 91786-5660
909-985-2785

Men's Abuse Survivors' Group
UCLA Psychology Clinic
Los Angeles, CA 90024
213-825-2305

Sex Crimes
San Jose, CA 95112
408-277-4102

Sexual Abuse Recovery Center
6540 Lusk Blvd.
San Diego, CA 92121-2766
619-450-3250

Sexual Assault Awareness Program
324 S. Palo Cedro Dr.
Diamond Bar, CA 91765-1501
909-861-1546

Colorado

Abuse Recovery Center
9334 W. 58th Ave.
Arvada, CO 80002-2002
303-424-2555

National Resource Center on Child Abuse and Neglect
63 Iverness Drive East
Englewood, CO 80112
800-227-5242

Sex Crimes
Colorado Springs, CO 80903
719-444-7540

Connecticut

Rape and Sexual Abuse Crisis Center
1845 Summer St.
Stamford, CT 06905-5017
203-348-9346

Sexual Assault Crisis Services
48 Howe St.
New Haven, CT 06511-4606
203-624-2273

Sexual Trauma Center
139 E. Center St.
Manchester, CT 06040-5242
860-643-1166

District of Columbia

Center for Abuse Recovery Empowerment
The Psychiatric Institute of Washington, DC
4228 Wisconsin Ave., N.W.
Washington, DC 20016
800-369-2273

Child Welfare League of America (CWLA)
440 1st St. NW, Suite 310
Washington, DC 20001
202-638-2952

National Clearinghouse on Child Abuse and Neglect Information
PO Box 1182
Washington, DC 20013-1182
800-394-3366

Rape, Abuse And Incest National Network
252 10th St., N.E.
Washington, DC 20002-6214
202-544-1034

Florida

Abuse Prevention Task Force
Fort Walton Beach, FL 32548
904-833-3948

Sex Crimes
Jacksonville, FL 32202
904-630-2168

Sexual Abuse Services
934 11th St. N.
Saint Petersburg, FL 33705-1205
813-898-5414

Georgia

Sexual Abuse Prevention Training and Education
Big Brothers Big Sisters of Metro Atlanta
100 Edgewood Ave., Suite 710
Atlanta, GA 30303
404-527-7600

Hawaii

Sex Abuse Treatment Center
1415 Kalakaua Ave., #201
Honolulu, HI 96826-1920
808-973-9337

Sexual Assault Crisis Center
Box #1278
Wailuku, HI 96793-6278
808-242-4335

Sexual Assault Treatment Program
Lihue, HI 96766
808-245-4144

Idaho

Sexual Abuse Now Ended
1716 S Roosevelt St.
Boise, ID 83705-2824
208-345-1170

Sexual Abuse Resource Center Inc.
Boise, ID 83704
208-375-7188

Illinois

International Society for Prevention of Child Abuse and Neglect (ISPCAN)
332 S. Michigan Ave., Suite 1600
Chicago, IL 60604
312-663-3520

National Committee for Prevention of Child Abuse
332 S. Michigan Ave., Suite 1600
Chicago, IL 60604-4357
800-835-2671

Sexual Abuse Victims Education
716 N Church St.
Rockford, IL 61103-6917
815-965-5172

Sexual Assault & Abuse Services
12 Health Services Drive
DeKalb, IL 60115-9637
(815) 758-7922

Sexual Assault Counseling and Information
Charleston, IL 61920
217-348-7666

Sexual Assault Prevention
510 Maine St.
Quincy, IL 62301-3941
217-223-2030

Indiana

Sex Crimes
Indianapolis, IN 46203
317-327-3330

Sex Offense Services
403 E. Madison St.
South Bend, IN 46617-2322
219-289-4357

Sexual Assault Recovery Project
Valparaiso, IN 46383
219-465-3408

Iowa

Domestic/Sexual Assault Outreach Center
PO Box 173
Fort Dodge, IA 50501
515-573-8000

Sexual Assault Advocacy Program
119 Sycamore, Medical Arts Bldg.
2nd Floor
Muscatine, IA 52761
319-263-8080

Sexual Assault Intervention Program—YWCA
318 5th St. S.E.
Cedar Rapids, IA 52401
319-363-5490

Kentucky

Abuse, Neglect, Adults and Children
Courthouse Square Campton, KY 41301
606-668-3101

Maryland

Sex Offense Task Force
Baltimore, MD 21202
410-396-5040

Survivors of Incest Anonymous
PO Box 26870
Baltimore, MD 21212
Phone (410) 433-2365

Michigan

Sexual Abuse Survivors Anonymous
Grosse Pointe, MI 48236
313-882-9646

Sexual Assault Recovery Assistance
Howell, MI 48843
517-548-4228

Minnesota

Rape And Abuse Crisis Center
115 5th St.
N Breckenridge, MN 56520-1420
218-643-6110

Sexual Abuse Survivors Service Inc.
Box #591
Albert Lea, MN 56007-0591
507-373-3655

Sexual Violence Center
2100 Pillsbury Ave.
Minneapolis, MN 55404-2347
612-871-5111

Mississippi

Sexual Recovery Center
1421 N State St., #403
Jackson, MS 39202-1658
601-353-9914

Missouri

Rape and Abuse Crisis Service
Jefferson City, MO 65101
314-634-4911

Rape Crisis And Sexual Abuse Center
943 N Boonville Ave.
Springfield, MO 65802-3801
417-863-7273

Sex Crimes
Saint Louis, MO 63102
314-444-5385

New Jersey

Sexual Abuse and Assault Program
4700 Long Beach Blvd.
Beach Haven, NJ 08008-3926
609-494-1090

Society's League Against Molestation (SLAM)
c/o Women Against Rape/Childwatch
PO Box 346
Collingswood, NJ 08108
609-858-7800

New Mexico

Incest Survivors Resource Network International (ISRNI)
PO Box 7375
Las Cruces, NM 88006
Phone (505) 521-4260

New York

Abuse and Assault Hotline
Oswego, NY 13126
315-342-1600

Partnerships for Survival (PFS)
Providing Coping Strategies for
Sexual Abuse Survivors
353 North Country Rd.
Smithtown, NY 11787
516-265-7202
Fax: 576-265-8676

Sex Crimes And Special Victims
Brooklyn, NY 11201
718-522-8855

Victim Services
2 Lafayette St.
New York NY 10007
Incest Helpline: 212-227-3000 or 212-227-3001
Headquarters: 212-577-7700
Fax: 212-385-0331

North Dakota

Abuse and Rape Crisis Center
Grand Forks, ND 58201
701-746-8900

Abuse Resource Network
409 4th Ave. W.
Lisbon, ND 58054
701-683-5061

Abused Persons Outreach Center
117 3rd St. NW
Valley City, ND 58072-2900
701-845-0072

Ohio

Abuse Recovery Counseling
3620 N. High St.
Columbus, OH 43214-3611
614-268-5778

Oregon

Abuse Investigation
133 S.E. 2nd Ave.
Hillsboro, OR 97123-4026
503-640-3489

Abuse Recovery
1030 River Bend Rd. N.W.
Salem, OR 97304-2110
503-370-8979

Sexual Abuse Clinic
8332 SE 13th Ave.
Portland, OR 97202-7100
503-238-1632

Sexual Abuse Intervention Project
4524 NE Hancock St.
Portland, OR 97213-1442
503-257-2558

Pennsylvania

Sexual Trauma and Recovery Program
929 Glenbrook Ave.
Bryn Mawr, PA 19010-2505
610-525-2027

Rhode Island

Abuse Control Through Education
3649 Post Rd., #9
Warwick, RI 02886-7237
401-738-1710

Survivor Connections
52 Lyndon Rd.
Cranston, RI 02905-1121
401-941-2548

Tennessee

Rape and Sexual Abuse Center
2120 Old Ashland City Rd.
Clarksville, TN 37043-4907
615-647-3632

Sexual Assault Crisis Center
PO Box 11523
Knoxville, TN 37939-1523
423-522-7273

Texas

Sex Crimes
715 E. 8th St.
Austin, TX 78701-3300
512-480-5026

Sexual Abuse Treatment Center
3131 Eastside St.
Houston, TX 77098-1919
713-520-8137

Utah

Sex Crimes
Salt Lake City, UT 84111
801-799-3420

Virginia

Abuse Program
1500 London Blvd.
Portsmouth, VA 23704-2132
804-393-8040

Sex Crimes
Newport News, VA 23607
804-247-8706

Washington

Abuse Counseling Service
721 D Ave., #206
Snohomish, WA 98290-2367
360-568-2988

Center for the Prevention of Sexual and Domestic Violence
1914 North 34th St.
Suite 105
Seattle WA 98103
206-631-1903

Sex Offender Treatment Service
212 W. 13th St.
Vancouver, WA 98660-2906
360-750-9893

Sexual Abuse Survivors' Association
5404 Meridian Ave. N.
Seattle, WA 98103-6139
206-526-2959

Wisconsin

Abused Men's Hotline
Madison, WI 53705
608-233-3317

Sexual Abuse Services
225 S. Hickory St.
Fond Du Lac, WI 54935-4830
414-923-1411

Chapter Notes

Chapter 1

1. Jeffrey J. Haugaard and N. Dickon-Reppucci, *The Sexual Abuse of Children* (San Francisco: The Jossey-Bass Publishers, 1988).

2. David Finkelhor, *Sexually Victimized Children* (New York: Free Press, 1979).

3. Ibid.

4. Robin Lenett, Dana Barthelme, and Bob Crane, *Sometimes It's O.K. to Tell Secrets* (New York: Tom Doherty & Associates, 1986).

5. Finkelhor.

6. Haugaard and Dickon-Reppucci.

7. Mic Hunter, *Abused Boys: The Neglected Victims of Sexual Abuse* (New York: Fawcett Columbine/ Ballentine, 1990).

8. Haugaard and Dickon-Reppucci.

Chapter 2

1. David Finkelhor, *Child Sexual Abuse* (New York: Free Press, 1984), in Teresa DeCrescenzo, ed. *Helping Gay and Lesbian Youth: New Policies, New Programs, New Practice* (Binghamton, N.Y.: Harrington Park Press, 1994).

Chapter 3

1. B. Groth, *Child Sexual Abuse* (Milwaukee: Milwaukee Women's Center, December 1995), Handout.

Chapter 4

1. Eric Marcus, *Is It a Choice?* (San Francisco: Harper, 1996).

2. N. Buhrich, J. Bailey, and N. Martin, "Sexual Orientation, Sexual Identity, and Sex-dimorphic Behaviors in Male Twins," *Behavior Genetics*, 1991.

3. D. Durby, "Gay, Lesbian and Bisexual Youth," in Teresa DeCrescenzo, ed. *Helping Gay and Lesbian Youth: New Policies, New Programs, New Practice* (Binghamton, N.Y.: Harrington Park Press, 1994).

4. B. Groth, *Child Sexual Abuse* (Milwaukee: Milwaukee Women's Center, December 1995), Handout.

Chapter 5

1. Dan Rather, "Sexual Predator Laws," CBS Evening News, with Dan Rather, November 1995.

2. Children's Forensic Institute, Sexually Abused Children's Bill of Rights (Washington, D.C.: 1990).

Chapter 6

1. B. Groth, *Child Sexual Abuse* (Milwaukee: Milwaukee Women's Center, December 1995), Handout.

2. Ibid.

Further Reading

Children's Forensic Institute. *Sexually Abused Children's Bill of Rights*. Washington, D.C., 1990.

DeCrescenzo, Teresa, ed. *Helping Gay and Lesbian Youth: New Policies, New Programs, New Practice*. New York: Harrington Park Press, 1994.

Finkelhor, David. *Sexually Victimized Children*. New York: Free Press, 1979.

Groth, B. *Child Sexual Abuse*. Handout. Milwaukee: Milwaukee Women's Center, 1995.

Haugaard, Jeffrey J. and N. Dickon-Reppucci. *The Sexual Abuse of Children*. The Jossey-Bass Social and Behavioral Science Series. San Francisco: Jossey-Bass Publishers, 1988.

Hunter, Mic. *Abused Boys*. New York: Fawcett Columbine/Ballentine, 1990.

Lenett, Robin, Dana Barthelme, and Bob Crane. *Sometimes It's O.K. to Tell Secrets*. New York: Tom Doherty & Associates, 1986.

Marcus, Eric. *Is It a Choice?* San Francisco: Harper, 1996.

Index